Blessings!
Jandi

NUGGETS
from Heaven

How to Receive More
Pearls of Wisdom from Above

Sandi Grove

Table of Contents

Introduction

The Night My Dad Went to Heaven

The pounding on the door ripped me out of my dream back into reality. The clock on the nightstand said 3:00 a.m. My stepmother yelled, "I need Sandi! Your dad is dead!" Gloria was crying and trembling. I flew out of my bed and ran into the guestroom. I jumped on the bed next to my dad and placed my hands on his face. "Wake up Dad!" No response. He was pale and life-less. I screamed for my husband to call 911. The operator told me to move my dad to the floor and begin CPR. My dad was a big guy, around 240 pounds. My husband, Corey, told the operator he was beyond resuscitation. I kept thinking, "This can't be happening." We were just snorkeling with my dad in Maui. "How could he be dead?"

June 6, 2009 started out as a typical Saturday around the Grove household. With three kids ages 12, 9, and 7, our lives were full to the brim with our kids' activities. My dad and Gloria, my stepmother of 36 years, loved it all. We all cheered as Cameron, our 12-year-old, threw a touchdown pass to Ryan, our nine-year-old, in their flag-football game. My dad watched Ryan throw three shut-out innings in his little league game. That Saturday night, Corey barbe-cued as we danced to Jimmy Buffett on the patio. After dinner, we went out for frozen yogurt. My dad asked Cameron to make him a hot-fudge sundae. When Cameron presented the sundae, my dad handed him a $20 bill as a tip. That $20 bill hangs over Cameron's bed to this day. As I type this I'm smiling, realizing the last thing my dad ate on this Earth was Cameron's hot fudge sundae.

The hours that followed felt like a weird, alternate reality, somewhere between real life and a dream state. About 10 police and firefighters filled the guestroom where my dad lay. I kept praying my kids would stay in their rooms. I did not want their last memory of their beloved grandpa to be this lifeless shell. By some miracle, all three kids stayed in their rooms all night long.

When the chaplain from the police department arrived, we climbed up on the king size bed and held hands in a circle around my dad. We prayed over him and asked God to take him home. The conversation that followed will stay with me forever. It was the first sign I received from my dad that told me everything was going to be ok. The chaplain told me he was also a 70-year-old man, and if he could write a script for how he would like to leave this Earth, it would be exactly like my dad. In that moment, I remembered how much my dad despised hospitals and illness. He died happy, full, and at peace. Perhaps I was blessed with the privilege of providing a com-fortable place for him to take his final breath.

When I called my dear friend and neighbor, Monica, she immediately walked across the street in her cream bathrobe. She mostly listened and cried as I shared what had transpired in my home that evening. But what she did tell me was that most people never get to have a dad like mine. And I got him for 41 years. This simple sentence changed my perception from what I had lost to what I had received.

You never know how you will react in this type of situation. For some reason I started baking candy bar pizza as the long hours ticked by. I described in detail the instructions to the police officer sitting at my kitchen counter. He wanted to share the recipe with his wife. How strange it must have been for all of the people who would come to my home that early morning to smell the aroma of freshly baked chocolate chip cookies. Looking back it seems strangely appropriate, since my dad was a notorious cookie monster, his favorite being chocolate chip.

The rest of that Sunday was surreal. As I watched my husband Corey help carry the blanket down the stairs that held my beloved father, I remember thinking how hard that must have been for him. My dad was a second father to him.

The following week was the last week of school. I went through the motions, but I know I was in a state of shock. I just couldn't believe I wouldn't see my dad again until I left this planet. It is comforting knowing he will be waiting for me with those big blue eyes and huge smile.

A strange thing happened on Tuesday morning. A woman named Barbara, who has a gift for communicating messages from our angels and loved ones in Heaven, called me and said she had an unexpected cancellation for the very next day. She said she had a feeling I needed to talk to her. She couldn't have been more right. I knew my dad was trying to get through to me. When I heard her lovely, grandmotherly voice, I was immediately overcome with emotion. I shared with her all that I had been through in the last several months and days. Six weeks before this my step-father lost a twelve year battle with prostate cancer. Now, losing my dad as well felt overwhelming. She told me my dad was there with her, with his "big, blue, watery eyes." His beloved Grandma Gray and little dog Coco were with him. He always told me stories about his grandmother, how she would rock him in her rocking chair. It gave me so much peace knowing she was with my dad. He chose my home for his final exit because he felt safe and loved, and he knew we would take care of Gloria.

June 6, 2009 was the beginning of a new era in my life. Although my spiritual journey did not begin there, it went to a new level. My stepmother and I began a pilgrimage of sorts. Just like so many who have lost their loved ones, we wanted to stay connected to my dad. We read as many books on Heaven as we could. We talk about my dad every day. I have learned more in the past seven years about the spiritual world than I have in my 41 years prior.

I pray his story, our story, will be a blessing to you. It truly does not end when our physical bodies die. For me, losing someone close to me changed the way I lived. Life is finite. There are only so many grains of sand in the hourglass. Once the last one passes, school is out. Let's learn our lessons before that final bell rings.

This book is my offering to you. It is a collection of the best "Nuggets" I have received since my dad's transition to Heaven. Each chapter illuminates a different lesson I have learned on my journey. May these Nuggets bless you in your life.

-Sandi

My Favorite Poem

I PROMISE MYSELF

To be so strong that nothing can disturb my peace of mind.
To talk health, happiness, and prosperity to every person I meet.
To make all my friends feel that there
is something worthwhile in them.
To look at the sunny side of everything and
make my optimism come true.
To think only of the best, to work only for the best,
and to expect only the best.
To be just as enthusiastic about the
success of others as I am about my own.
To forget the mistakes of the past and press on to
the greater achievements of the future.
To wear a cheerful expression at all times and give
a smile to every living creature I meet.
To give so much time to improving myself that
I have no time to criticize others.

To be too large for worry, too noble for anger, too strong for fear,
and too happy to permit the presence of trouble.
To think well of myself and proclaim this fact to the world,
not in loud words but in great deeds.
To live in the faith that the whole world is on my side.
So long as I am true to the best that is in me.

Christian D. Larson

Part 1 | NUGGETS 101

What is a Nugget From Heaven?

A Nugget from Heaven is any kind of divine information you receive. It could be an actual physical sign, an idea that just pops in your mind, an intuitive feeling, or a dream. Nuggets from Heaven come from your heart space rather than your head space. I have been receiving Nuggets from Heaven since I was a young child. I can remember being six years old in the upstairs bathroom of my home. I remember staring in the mirror and knowing on some very deep, intuitive level that I was much more than the blond haired, blue-eyed, freckle-faced girl looking back at me. I can actually remember thinking, "So this is who I chose to be this time." I still have those surreal, out-of-body type moments from time to time. It's like my inner spirit is peeking her head out just for a moment.

My mom started taking me to church when I was about 10 years old. I learned that Jesus taught that if we ask we will receive, and so I started asking and never stopped. I can remember asking for it to rain so that my softball game would be cancelled, because I had birthday party I wanted to attend. Even though no rain was forecast, it rained. I pray for everything and find often times the answer is yes. I pray for small things from help finding the perfect gift for a friend or the speedy recovery of a loved one in the hospital. I write out my prayers every morning when I wake up, which is usually around 5:30 a.m. When a friend tells me about something she is going through in her life, I start praying even as she is speaking. I love praying out loud with my friends. We often hike to the top of a mountain, hold hands in a circle, and pray for a friend going through a challenging time. People are so touched when you tell them you are praying for them. It's one of the best gifts you can give, and it doesn't cost a dime.

When someone tells me a prayer request has been answered, this is a wonderful Nugget from Heaven. What better confirmation is there than to see our prayers manifest right before our eyes.

Another way God and our angels try to communicate with us, or shower us with divine Nuggets, is through signs. One of the most powerful signs I have received happened one night as I was getting into the bathtub. I had been reading a book about guardian angels, and I had this overwhelming feeling of embarrassment when I realized my guardian angels had witnessed everything I had ever done wrong for my entire life. But just as I had that thought, another even more powerful thought came over me: My angels loved me unconditionally. They completely supported me and were cheering me on every moment of my life. With that thought, I noticed my son's little toy fish on the side of the bathtub wiggling back and forth. I will never forget that moment. I picked up the fish, looked at it, and then put it back down. I tried to think of any logical reason the fish would have moved. My son had not been in the tub that night, so there was no possibility of some sort of built up water pressure. Then I remembered what I was thinking about right before the fish moved, and I knew my angels were screaming, "Yes! Yes! That is exactly how we feel about you!" They didn't want me to feel guilty or embarrassed, only loved and supported unconditionally. That is their job. Period.

After my dad died, the signs I received went to a whole new level. Realizing that my dad was at peace helped me move from feeling like a victim to feeling blessed to be his daughter. When we are cloaked in grief, it is extremely difficult for our loved ones to give us signs.

Sunday, the day after my dad went to Heaven, my son Cameron had a playoff baseball game. We decided to go to the game. My dad would have wanted Cameron to play. I knew my dad was at the game when Cameron got a great hit to right field (he always hit to left). Both of our boys won the championship for their divisions the following Monday. It was the first and last time that ever happened to either of them. On the way home from the ball field, I asked my dad out loud if he could get my CD player working. It had been broken for almost a year. Miraculously it worked! Not only that, but the song that came on was Highway 20 Ride by Zac Brown Band. It's a song that reminds me of the drive my dad made every other weekend for my entire childhood for bimonthly visits with me and my brother (my parents were divorced when I was four). Even to this day, I can't hear it without picturing my dad.

The signs kept coming, and I loved and appreciated every single one. It made me feel closer to my dad than ever. I knew he was watching over us. One Saturday afternoon Corey was trying to get down a bird's nest from the top of one of our stereo speakers in the outdoor cabana. We had to leave to take one of our sons to his baseball game. When we got back from the game, the nest was lying perfectly intact in the middle of the cabana floor with the broom lying next to it! I immediately knew this was a funny sign from my dad, since he had tried to get a bird's nest down at our previous home. In that situation, about 20 birds descended upon him. As he was running back into the house, he tripped and cut his knee, tumbling inside as the birds continued to dive bomb him. We all stood in the kitchen watching this hysterical scene, laughing but concerned that he was ok.

When I share my dad's story, people open up and share their similar "sign stories." It's amazing how many people receive signs from their loved ones in Heaven. One man shared with me that his father died on the Fourth of July. He said he sees the numbers 7 and 4 together almost every day, and he always knows it's a nod from his father. Another one of my friends lost her dear grandfather when she was 12 years old. We were in a bar watching the San Francisco Giants playoff game at the time. It didn't look good for our Giants at that point. They were down and needed to win this game or they would be out of the World Series. Everyone who knew baseball said they didn't have a chance. I asked her if she had ever asked her grandfather for a sign. She had not, and so right there in that crowded bar I grabbed her hands and asked her grandfather to give her a sign. The Giants came back and won that game as well as the series. They proceeded to win three more World Series over the next six years!

Another dear friend of mine lost her dad recently to a long fight with cancer. Just as he was passing, my friend noticed two hummingbirds playing just outside the window. A few days after he died, a hummingbird flew into my friend's house at 9:00 at night. She has received many more hummingbird signs. A few months later, her youngest daughter went to sleep away camp for the first time. Naturally she was randomly assigned to the Hummingbird Cabin. This may all sound like coincidences, but when you receive so many signs, eventually you start to accept and understand that our loved ones don't cease to exist. They desperately want us to know that they are doing great. They want to help us in any way they can.

Sometimes Nuggets from Heaven are simple thoughts or ideas that seem to come out of nowhere. I get these quite often when I am walking or hiking in nature. It's almost as if I am receiving a lecture or seminar on a particular topic that's relevant to my life at that moment. On one particular night I couldn't sleep as I lay worrying about one of my children. In that moment, I pictured a little girl lifting her hands over her head as Nuggets (which looked like little red hearts) showered down on her. (This is actually where the words "Nuggets From Heaven" came from.) It was in this powerful moment that I released the burden of my children's souls to God. My job was to shine my light. There was no gift I could give my children that would help them more than the example of a mother doing what she came here to do. I felt such relief. I didn't consciously realize I felt responsible for their souls until I released that burden. I decided I wanted a physical manifestation of this Nugget from Heaven, so the next day I went to the art store and bought a small, square canvas and painted it black. I then made a little girl out of white clay and stretched her arms above her head. I love this piece of art and have it displayed prominently in my kitchen as a constant reminder to lift my worries to Heaven.

CHALLENGE # 1

Think about your life up to this point. Think of a specific Nugget from Heaven you have received.

Nugget:

How Do I Get Me Some?

There are many, many ways to receive more Nuggets from Heaven in your life. God and your angels want to shower you with Nuggets. The very first thing I do when I wake up in the morning is I stretch my arms up to the sky and say silently or out loud, "Thank you God. Bless me and use me today." This simple sentence is incredibly powerful. It starts my day with positive momentum. The habits you have in the morning have tremendous impact on the trajectory of your day. Have you ever had one of those mornings where everything seems to go wrong from the spilled coffee, burnt toast, and fighting kids? Now picture a morning where everything is easy and peaceful. Notice how this feels in your body. When the very first words you speak are words of gratitude and a desire to bless and be a blessing, expectation theory says you have a very good chance of success. Just try this tomorrow morning and see how the day goes.

The second habit I use daily is my writing practice. I set a timer on my kitchen oven for 11 minutes. Not only do I write out what

I am most thankful for, I also lift up prayer requests for others. I pray for upcoming events in my life like travel or a meeting I have that day. Finally, I write "In my dream world ... " I love this part of my prayer because the sky is literally the limit. I write about my life in the present tense, as if I have already received the blessings I am requesting. For example, each morning I write, "I am a New York Times best-selling author. God speaks through me to millions of people and helps them live more authentic and spiritually connected lives." I also write simple affirmations like, "I prepare healthy, delicious, creative dinners for my family every night. Family dinner is fun, and everyone participates in the conversation." Whatever excites you or lights you up, write it. You're creating your life in these 11 minutes. Create a good one. The writing system I use is called Vimala. I strongly recommend Vimala Rodgers's book How Your Handwriting Can Change Your Life. Both Tony Robbins and Louise Hay adopted her writing system and saw huge changes in their lives. If you are reading this right now thinking it's totally unrealistic, then I challenge you to start small. Baby steps are sometimes the best way to incorporate new habits into our lives. Simply commit to writing two words every morning: "Thank you." Actually write them down. Even if you grab an opened bill and write on the envelope, something about writing the words is powerful.

The third habit I use daily to open the Nugget floodgate is to bless my food. I eat and prepare almost all of my own meals. When I sit down at my kitchen table to eat a meal, I always take a moment and thank God, the soil, and the sun for the food I am about to consume. I ask that God bless the food to my body. I believe something miraculous happens to the food when we do this. I slow down and absorb the scenery around me. The entire eating experience changes when I bless my food. I am also more in tune with what my body needs when I bless my food. I listen and stop eating when I am satisfied. I prepare food that my body is craving. The messages our bodies give us are very important Nuggets. Our bodies are extremely wise. They know exactly what we need. We just need to quiet our minds so that we can hear.

Music is another powerful tool to open the flow of divine Nuggets. Albert Einstein was listening to Mozart when the theory of relativity was literally downloaded to him. Music connects with our spirits in a way nothing else can. When we are feeling negative emotions like stress or worry, we are unable to hear our angels' voices whispering. When we listen to a soothing peace of music, it relaxes us and opens us up. In my home, I noticed whenever Zac Brown Band was playing, my teenage son's mood changed immediately. He was lighter and happier. In the morning I have Mozart and Vivaldi playing as my kids get ready for school. The atmosphere in my home in the morning is always calm and peaceful. I play certain kinds of music in the car when my kids are crabby and I immediately notice a change in mood. One time as I was driving back from a dance competition with my daughter and I put on the Disney Pandora station. We were both immediately transported back to her childhood with songs from The Lion King, Mary Poppins and Beauty and the Beast. It was the best drive! Angels love music and are drawn to the high vibration it provides.

Thinking good-feeling thoughts attracts divine Nuggets. Our angels want to help us, but when we cloak ourselves in negative thoughts they are unable to get through because angels exist on a higher frequency. The more we are disciplined about our thoughts and only allow positive, uplifting thoughts to fill our head space, the more fun our angels can have with us. If you notice you are in a negative downward spiral, distract yourself with something that feels good as early as possible when it's easier to change your momentum. If you think a negative thought, don't share it out loud. Giving it attention automatically makes it grow, like watering weeds. Treat negative thoughts and feelings like a bear in the woods—back off slowly. I have a few "go to" strategies I use that help me change negative momentum. A warm, lavender bubble bath or a walk in nature with my dog both do the trick. Sometimes I do a guided meditation or simply take a nap to bring my mood up. You can also try tapping, which means you tap on different meridian points in your body while breathing deeply. George Smith, the creator of tapping, has over 600 YouTube videos that explain how to tap. This is a great process to teach kids. Try different strategies and see what works for you. The most important lesson is that you identify when you are in a negative downward spiral and you do something to slow down the momentum. This is incredibly important if you want to have a happy life led by the divine.

Daydreaming is a powerful tool to help you receive divine Nuggets. When you find yourself in a daydream, notice where you are. This is a picture of your potential future. You wouldn't be drawn to it if it weren't a strong potential path for you. God and your angels want you to live the life of your dreams. They will do everything in their power to support you in creating that life.

Did you know your physical mind can't tell the difference between a daydream and reality? The same neurons fire in your brain when you picture yourself skiing as when you are actually skiing. Make sure you don't spend time imagining negative scenarios. These have power too. Parents worry about their kids and don't realize when they picture the worst-case scenario they are actually giving that possibility more power. Write "In my dream world ... " and see what follows. Write anything that lights you up. Don't worry if it seems unrealistic. Anyone who has achieved their life goals had to ignore the voice in their head telling them the goal was too big and unachievable. You can do, be, or have anything you can create and see.

God and your angels have input for you on every action you take, including the food you eat and the items you buy. I find that when I am out of alignment with God, I make poor food and spending choices. Both eating and spending money are vibrational, so make sure you are feeing good before you put the fork in your mouth or pull out your wallet. Check in with your inner spirit by saying, "Will this food support and nourish me right now?" Before you make a purchase, say, "Will this item bring me joy?" Your inner spirit knows exactly what you need to eat to feel your very best. Your inner spirit knows the exact items that will support and bring you peace, beauty, and joy. If an item doesn't light you up, don't buy it. Period. It's not right, at least not in this moment. When you think of making a meal, spend some time imagining what sounds wonderful to your body. That is the meal to make. Ask your angels for help with a difficult conversation. When I was a Director of Human Resources, I would always spend a few minutes alone before an employee termination. I would ask for God and my angels to help me communicate this difficult message with love. Angels will even help you pick the right home or car for you. Just ask and wait for the signs. You can receive Nuggets that will save you thousands of dollars!

CHALLENGE # 2

Add one new habit to your life that brings you more Nuggets from Heaven. Either choose one of the habits covered here, or come up with your own. Do it every day, and write down the Nuggets as you receive them.

New Habit:

Raise It Up —
Your Vibration That Is

Picture yourself on a tropical beach. The warm, white sand feels great on your feet. You jump in the water and play in the waves. You body surf a few waves and then lie back in the salty water and let the ocean support you. You are totally in the moment, enjoying all of the sounds, sights, tastes, smells, and feelings in your body. How do you feel in your body right now? Simply picturing yourself frolicking in the waves can raise your vibration, even if it's the middle of winter in the Northeast. Raising your vibration is essential to receiving more divine Nuggets in your life. The better you feel, the more divinely guided your life will be. If you want to help others in your life, the best way to do it is through raising your own vibration. Your positive example is the best gift you can ever give the world.

The first and most powerful way to raise your vibration is through self-appreciation. You truly cannot give love to another if you aren't feeling love toward yourself. Think about your car. You do regular maintenance on your car. You change the oil and the tires.

You wash it regularly and keep it tidy. How much more important is your body than your car? How are you treating the vehicle God lent you for this journey? Are you thinking positive, uplifting thoughts? Are you feeding your body high vibrational foods like organic fruits and vegetables? Are you drinking lots of pure water? Are you listening to the cues your body gives you or is your mind telling your body to pipe down? What happens when your car starts making a weird sound and you continue to ignore it? Typically there is a price to pay. The same is true for our bodies. Doing things that make our bodies feel good and thinking thoughts that make our souls sing is the first key to raising our vibration. Positive affirmations are extremely powerful if used often throughout your day. I write out several affirmations every morning like, "I am part of a close, tight, good-to-each-other family." "I am incredibly fit." "I am aligned with God." "I give something to every person I interact with today." "I use my gifts to help millions of people live more spiritually connected, authentic lives." "I receive unexpected gifts, signs, and miracles today." When your mind starts to wander to a negative place, immediately rein it in and replace those thoughts with one of your affirmations. It's also a good idea to have your affirmations written on notecards placed in prominent locations you view often like your bathroom mirror or refrigerator. The best way to manifest a body you love is to think positive, good-feeling thoughts toward your current body. Send love to the parts of your body you detest and watch the miracle unfold. I did this toward my belly pooch. After giving birth to three children, my lower abdomen didn't quite look the same. I decided to send it love and thank that part of my body for doing its job of holding those precious babies for nine months. Now I love that part of my body. It reminds me of how blessed I am to have three amazing kids.

Sharing your unique gifts and passion is the second way to raise your personal vibration. Picture being invited to a dear friend's home for a dinner party. Let's say you spend the day preparing a delicious dish to share. Naturally you would place the dish in a prominent place so that everyone could partake. The same is true when we share our gifts with the world. Whatever it is that lights you up, that is your gift to share. Trust your own excitement. Ignore the voice in your head that says, "But how can I pay my mortgage writing children's books? " If God put the desire or dream in you, your job is to simply follow your passion and share your gift with the world. Every truly gifted artist, author, musician, and inventor follows his or her passion regardless of the plethora of reasons to quit. A mom on my son's basketball team shared with me a simple but profound thought at a team party. She said her teenage kids had just gotten back from a leadership camp where they learned that if you don't share your gift with the world, there could be hundreds or even thousands of people that don't share their gift. You never know how far and wide your gift can spread. When I get that little whisper to reach out to someone, I don't question it. I simply listen and obey.

Another way to raise your vibration is through prayer. It's impossible to pray and worry at the same time. When I pray, I lift up my burdens and immediately feel a weight lifted from me. I pray very specifically for the people in my life, knowing that if the answer is no, then God's plan was better than mine. But prayer is powerful. I pray for God's healing love and light to soothe and calm loved ones going through challenges. I pray for blessings upon my children for success in school and sports, for safety, and happiness. If I go on a trip I always pray for easy travel, great weather, and beautiful moments. When I walk my dog in the morning, I ask for a blessing upon every house on my street. If I am in a large meeting, I silently ask for a blessing upon every person in the room. The interesting thing that happens when you pray for complete strangers is they don't feel like strangers anymore. Immediately you get the sense that we truly are one. What is good for them is good for me. Nothing seals that on my soul like prayer.

A fourth strategy for raising your vibration is to follow your passion in each moment. This simply means do the thing that sounds the best to you right now. When you are trying to decide what to wear in the morning or what to eat for breakfast, follow this strategy. You can use this when planning a trip to a vacation destination or a trip to the grocery store. At work, follow this strategy and you will produce original, passionate ideas that are difference makers. Thinking in an out-of-the-box, creative way is always highly desirable in the workforce. When we follow our passions, even down to the smallest detail, God and our angels are able to work through us. When you raise your vibration (and following your passion does this), you are closer to Divine vibration, and this is where serendipity and synchronicity become commonplace. Our intuition becomes heightened and solutions to problems flow easily to us. Have you ever struggled with a problem to no avail and then walked away? While showering or hiking or washing the dishes, the solution pops into your head. This is a great example of why we shouldn't focus our energies on the problem but rather on what lights us up, and the problem will be solved with the least amount of energy and struggle.

A few winters ago we had huge rainstorms that produced excessive water flowing down our street. There were some sandbags in the gutters that caused the water to flow way out around them. It reminded me of the sandbags we have in our thinking. A sandbag is anything that trips up your positive vibration. It's a topic you focus on that brings you stress and worry. It's important to identify your own sandbags. It could be negative thoughts about your body, judgment toward a family member, jealousy toward friends, etc. Even excessive worrying about children can be a sandbag. These thoughts are like a big, hairy monster you invite into your living room. How do you get rid of it? Simply ignore it. Don't give it air time or thought time. We spend way too much time on negative topics. When you find yourself stuck on a sandbag, try to change the channel in your mind as soon as possible. The longer you focus on the stressful, negative topic, the harder it will be to raise your vibration. When someone close to you has a low vibration, the best thing you can do to help them is keep your vibration high. If you sink down to their level, it's like jumping in to save a drowning person rather than throwing them a life preserver. I have learned from having three teenagers, the most effective strategy I can use to help them is to pray for them every morning. I envision them happy, healthy, and successful. I write out a few sentences for each of my children. I know somewhere deep inside they love knowing I am praying for them.

Think of your vibration or mood as a flame burning inside of you. Don't let things outside of you touch your flame. The great masters all knew this habit. Nelson Mandela said he was grateful for his 27-year imprisonment because it helped him get right in his head. There is always something to be grateful for in every moment. We just need to train our minds to focus on it.

I have several "go to" vibrational uppers I use when I find myself paddling against the current. Warm baths, hiking or walking my dog and meditating always lift my vibration. Have a toolbox of vibrational uppers that you can use whenever you notice your mood is starting to descend. If all else fails, take a nap. Our vibration naturally comes back up when we sleep.

CHALLENGE # 3

Write a list of vibrational uppers that you can use when you feel your mood dropping.

You Don't Have to Go It Alone

(Divine Helpers Surround You Constantly)

Do you know that you are constantly surrounded by divine entities? Their singular purpose it to love, support and assist you on your journey. It's unfortunate that most people never call upon these powerful entities or acknowledge these divine beings in any way. You can start your relationship with your divine support team by tapping into your own soul. Next, you can develop a relationship with your loved ones in Heaven. Finally, your life will miraculously transform when you learn to connect with your angels.

Each and every one of us holds the flame of God, and together we are God's light and love. It is not outside of us, but within us. We have to be authentically ourselves to do our part in completing the puzzle. We have to do what lights us up and makes our heart sing in each moment. If there are circumstances you don't like in your life right now, you have to change You, and the world around you will change. When you change, even by sending a blessing or prayer, you change the world.

Find a time each day to connect with your soul. Some people like to spend a few minutes before going to bed reviewing the blessings of their day. Other people find a few moments throughout the day to quiet their mind and check in.

CHALLENGE # 4

What is the best time of day for you to connect with your soul?

Our loved ones in Heaven want desperately to help and support us here on Earth. They have seen the light, and they want us to live our lives with joy, appreciation, and fun. When they see us cloaked in grief, they understand, but they know we are wasting our precious moments. When we are looking for signs from our loved ones, we receive them. There are several ways our loved ones in Heaven come through. Electronics are easy for spirits to manipulate. One woman shared with me that the clock on her oven which had been broken for 20 years, came on miraculously after her husband passed. The number on the clock was his birthday, and she immediately knew he was there with her. She desperately wanted him to stay, but after about 20 minutes the light went out. Another friend of mine had her alarm clock turn on by itself in the middle of the night after her dad went to Heaven. The alarm clock was off, but the radio turned on all by itself.

Animals, birds, and insects have the ability to deliver messages from our loved ones. One sign we received from the animal kingdom came when my stepmother, Gloria, was spreading my dad's ashes along the beach in San Diego. It was their favorite walking spot. My dad was a big guy, 6'3" and 240 pounds, so it took Gloria a few hours to lovingly sprinkle his remains along the serene coastline. When she finally finished, she looked out over the ocean and saw two dolphins swimming together. It was the perfect sign from my dad. Even though he was in Heaven, he was still with her. My daughter, who was eight at the time, painted a picture of this moment, which hangs in Gloria's house to this day.

I lost another friend to cancer named Dawn around the same time as my aunt. She left two beautiful daughters, 13 and 7. When I was doing my early morning solo hike to the top of a mountain, I asked my friend in Heaven if there was any thing I could do for her.

Immediately the book Embraced by the Light by Betty Eadie popped into my head. The book is about a woman who went to Heaven after she died and then came back to Earth to tell her story. It's the book that gave me the most comfort after my dad went to Heaven. I told Dawn that if she wanted me to send her 13-year-old daughter the book, I would need a sign. Within about 30 seconds I saw a deer run past me in the woods. I have never seen a deer before or since on that hike, which I do every week. I sent the book.

Pay attention to the numbers you see throughout the day because your loved ones may be trying to get messages to you through these numbers. A friend of mine recently lost her beloved golden retriever to cancer. A few weeks after putting her dog down, she bought several lottery tickets and picked three numbers for each ticket. For one of the tickets, she picked 131 because that was her dog's birthday. She won $550 dollars from that ticket. When she returned home and told her husband, he told her that was the exact amount they paid the vet to put their dog down. They both knew in that moment their beloved dog was reaching out to them from Heaven. Notice numbers on digital clocks. I see 11:11 quite a bit. Eleven is an angel number. I also see 6:21, which is my birthday. Always say "thank you " when you receive one of these number messages. When we thank our loved ones it inspires them to give us more.

From the day following my dad's transition to Heaven, I started finding objects that I knew were from him. The first thing I found was a soft cloth sunglasses case in perfect condition just lying in the street. The odd thing about this was I had been searching for one of these for several months and had been unable to find one anywhere. Somehow I knew my dad was already reaching out to me. One time I was walking to my car and talking to my dad about my teenage son, who I was particularly worried about at that time. I said, "Is he going to be alright, Dad?" In that exact moment, I looked down and saw a quarter. I picked it up, and the words I heard from my dad were, "He's going to be more than fine Sandi. He is going to be great! Look how good you came out." For some reason I had forgotten what a lost teenager I had been. Hearing my dad's voice and knowing that my son would be happy and successful in his life gave me incredible peace. The bonus was I knew my dad was watching over him.

One time I asked my dad for a sign right before I left for my morning walk with my dog Bella. Since my dad's name was Bud, I was literally searching high and low on license plates and street signs for his name. I finally stopped scouring every object I encountered and just started noticing the beauty of the nature surrounding me. Like everything else in life, we often get what we want when we loosen our grip and live in the moment. I immediately noticed hundreds of tiny "buds" on the trees lining the street. Ahhhh, he was there all the time.

Dreams are another way our loved ones communicate with us. It took several months for me to have my first dream with my dad. When I awaken from a dream with my dad, I always feel incredibly grateful and blessed. I actually feel like I had a visit from him, which I did. Three years after my dad passed, I had a very powerful, realistic dream. In the dream, my dad told me he would not be giving me tons of signs any more. I immediately understood that he would be here with me immediately if I called upon him, but his energy in Heaven was going to be focused elsewhere. The dream left me a bit sad because I adore and appreciate every sign I have ever received from my dad. But I was so thankful for that dream because, once again, it was confirmation that he had my back, even up in Heaven.

CHALLENGE # 5

Have you ever received a sign from a loved one in Heaven? If not, has anyone you know shared a sign they have received?

How would you like it if you had a team of incredibly wise, loving beings at your beck and call, following you around all day, every day? You could ask any one of these team members to help you with any problem, challenge, or situation you faced throughout your day. All 7 billion of us have exactly that. Angels watch over us every moment and wait for our call. When we call upon our angels, it's like turning their power switch on. They want to help us with everything from parking spaces to ending world hunger. Nothing is too small or too big for an angel. The more you ask, the more you receive.

The word "angel" means messenger of God. All major religions have angels. Our guardian angels are with us from the moment we are conceived until the moment we take our last breath. Angels have not lived in human form before, but they can manifest into human form temporarily in order to help us. One woman I know was visited by a nurse in the hospital right after she delivered her daughter. The woman was a teenager at the time, and she was planning on putting her daughter up for adoption. The nurse asked her to really search her heart and take a day to think about this decision. That night the woman heard the voice of God telling her to keep her daughter. When the woman went back to the hospital to thank the nurse, the hospital administration told her no such woman with her description worked at the hospital. In that moment, the woman knew she had received a visit from her angel. Her daughter turned out to be the greatest blessing in her life.

You can ask your guardian angels their names. I did this one time and a black panther showed up. I wanted an angel in a long white flowing gown. The panther quickly disappeared and my dream angel appeared. Our angels don't care what they look like. They simply want to help us. Trust the picture or name you receive, and try not to muster the image you want or think you should have. I have learned to appreciate and adore my black panther. She is fiercely protective, wise, and grounded.

CHALLENGE # 6

Close your eyes. Relax your entire body. Take several deep breaths.

Picture your guardian angel or spiritual guide. Trust the first picture that pops into your mind and write it down here.

Part 2 | LEFT HANDED NUGGETS

The summer of 2014 was a period of my life that will always stand out as unique and serendipitous. It began when my neighbor texted me one morning and asked me if I wanted to go receive a hug from a world famous healer named Ama. Even though I had lived in San Ramon (a suburb east of San Francisco) for 14 years, I had never heard of Ama, whose ashram was 10 minutes from my house. Supposedly one hug from Ama had dramatically changed people's lives. I was intrigued. I figured with my busy schedule of driving around three kids every day there was little chance I would be able to take six hours to stand in line to receive a hug that may or may not have any impact on my life. However, when I checked my schedule for the next day, it turned out that each of my kids had rides already scheduled, so I truly did have the day open. I took this as a sign that I should go to the ashram with my friend.

We arrived at the ashram around 7:30 a.m. We actually only had to stand in line until about 1:00. Oddly, the energy of the ashram was so peaceful and positive, the time just flew by. We met a yoga instructor from San Francisco who was standing in front of us. She told us that she took the BART train in from the city and just had faith that someone also visiting the ashram that morning would pick her up at the station. And of course someone did! Apparently the volunteers at the ashram encourage people who are driving their personal cars to stop by and pick up people from the BART station.

When it was finally my turn to receive my hug, I was a little nervous. I was told to hold an intention in my mind as I received my hug.

When this powerful, 4' 11" bundle of pure joy and love embraced me, my mind went blank. As I kneeled, my face awkwardly went straight into her belly so I was breathing in her rose oil. I was actually focusing on getting air through the white robe she was wearing. My friend had the same experience. We ate lunch at the ashram and then returned home. I didn't feel any different, but I was grateful for the experience. A few days later, both my friend and I came down with the exact same flu. It lasted about a week. I couldn't understand why I got sick right after my Ama hug. My friend shared with me that it's fairly common to get sick after visiting Ama if there are things in your life you need to purge. Apparently I had a quite a bit to purge. When I started to feel better, I began writing with my left hand each morning when I awoke. I've always spent time in prayer and journaling in the early morning hours, but this was a new practice that began right after my Ama encounter. I would clear my mind, pick up my pen, and just write whatever flowed into my mind. Sometimes I would ask a specific loved one in Heaven for advice. For example, I asked my Aunt Bobbi what she has learned since she went to Heaven. Other times I just opened myself up to whatever God and my angels had for me. I did this every morning for about two months, and then it just stopped. I believe my left-handed blogs are the blessing I received from my Ama hug. I have listed them here. I pray they bless you as they have blessed me.

Fun

(Aunt Bobbi)

It's supposed to be fun on Earth. We forget this as we grow into adults. Run barefoot in the wet grass. Lose yourself while gazing at a redwood tree, sunset, or the stars. Savor the delicious, creamy sweetness of an ice-cream cone. Get lost in the moment. Get rid of all negative emotion (worry, fear, judgment, etc.) and you can choose love, laughter, or peace instead. We waste so much precious time on frivolous things that don't matter. We accumulate so much stuff, and then our stuff is constantly calling us to organize it, use it, or get rid of it. All of which are time zappers. Be fully present in the moment you are living. Feel what you are feeling deeply. Notice sensations in your body. Your body is so wise. It knows exactly what it needs in each moment. It knows what to eat and how much. It knows which kind of exercise is best. One day it might need to run, another day walk, another day stretch, and another day rest. Just ask your body what it needs and then listen for the answer. Focus your mind on feeling appreciation for every blessing in your life big and small. Notice the warm greeting the checker gives you at the grocery store.

Pay attention to the birds singing first thing in the morning. Say and write, "Thank you" a lot, every chance you get. It will bring more of the good stuff your way. Spend more time thinking about the kind of person you would like to be. If you had a magic wand, would you be easier about things? More fit? Generous? A great dancer? A marathon runner? Would you speak a second language? Any characteristic you can visualize for yourself you can achieve. In fact, you are more than halfway there. Just spend some time each day fleshing out your fantasy or dream world and you will pull it into your reality. Your life is a gift. It's your gift to yourself and to the world. First you must fill yourself with loving, appreciative thoughts and feelings. By your example, you will positively impact everyone in your life. Vibrations are contagious. So make sure yours is a good one. Look for opportunities to help people every day. Whether it's holding a door open or smiling at a store clerk, your kind acts reverberate throughout the universe, and they come back to you ten fold.

Self-Healing

You can heal yourself by picturing yourself wrapped in the warm, cozy blanket of God's healing light and love. If you have a particular pain, take a few minutes to see yourself—better yet—feel yourself healthy, vibrant, and full of positive energy. If there are any persistent, negative relationships in your life deal with them head on. Figure out why you have chosen the path you have, and send love to the person challenging you. Even if the relationship ends, you will have learned what you needed to learn from the relationship, so you won't have to keep repeating it.

Do less, but do what you do with more of you—all of you—ideally. Whatever task you undertake, whether it be for work or pleasure, focus all of your thought in that moment. People miss so much of their lives simply by not paying attention to the moment they are in. And for goodness sake turn off all of those devices. The TVs, the laptops, and the phones are robbing you of your life. Technology can be used to send love, but don't let it monopolize your life.

When we come together, we physically impact each other simply by being next to each other. Take each opportunity you have in your short time here to send love to those around you. You can do this through words, actions, or even silent blessings and prayers. They will receive them all. When you are giving from a place of unconditional love, you are more attractive, radiant, healthy, and whole. You will positively impact everyone who comes in contact with you. In fact, the only way you can change somebody is by giving love and appreciation. People will feel the longing deep within themselves to do the same.

Criticism and complaining are wasting time and energy. Just turn away from the unpleasant thought. Turn the channel. Change the subject. Take a walk. Take a deep, full breath. Find three things you are grateful for. Now choose three more. Keep going until you feel God's love permeate every cell in your body. How about thanking your body, heart, lungs, liver, kidneys, eyes, ears, and skin? All do their jobs of taking orders from you without much, if any, thanks. The only time most of us appreciate our bodies is when we are sick. Our bodies try to tell us what they need, but we don't listen. We blame our body for being sick, tired, or fat. Can you imagine getting mad at your car for running out of oil and blowing the engine? The light was on, we just chose to ignore it. Stop ignoring the warning lights in your life. They are gifts from Heaven meant to help you.

Work

Many of us struggle when choosing our work. It's so easy. Just follow what lights you up. What do you daydream about? What do you like to talk to your friends about? What do you Google? What are you curious about and want to learn more about? For example, people who work at a nursery should love plants and love connecting the right plant with the right person. Follow your passion; it's never wrong. Trust God's plan. It's always better than yours.

Prepare Food with Love

Whenever you make food for yourself or someone else, make sure you bless the food and ask that the food bless the body of the person eating it. When you are choosing your food, examine the food lovingly, selecting the very freshest, most appealing option. The cells in the body of the consumer will recognize and respond to this loving treatment through an especially pleasing and satisfying physical and emotional sensation. Why do you think people feel so bad after eating fast food? The environment in which you eat is also extremely important. Never eat when you are experiencing any kind of negative emotion. Take a walk, a bath, or a nap, and release the bad feelings before returning to the table. If parents have negative feedback to discuss with their children, the family dinner table should not be the place to share it.

Aging

Feel good and grateful at every age. You only get one year of your whole life to be this age. Every year on your birthday say out loud, "This will be my best year yet!" When you begin to see changes in your body like smile lines, view them like a marathon runner views markers along his journey. Marathon runners aren't resentful that they have made it to mile 18, but rather grateful and proud. You can age beautifully by listening to your body, eating healthy, whole foods, drinking lots of pure water, and laughing and loving your way through each day. Be the exception, the example of how to age magnificently. It will be contagious. Know that 99.9 percent of everything is how you see it. See aging as fun and freeing. Your later years can be your best years if you take care of business when you are young. You have love to give, people to help, and a beautiful life to savor each day. God will call you home the moment your work is done. So don't worry about when or how you will die. Focus all of your energy on living well. Be full of enthusiasm at every age. The first thought you should think when you open your eyes in the morning is "Thank you!"

Stress

Stress is a physical toxin in your body. Of course a little stress can heighten performance, but we have incorporated an unhealthy amount of stress into our daily lives. This problem is easily fixed because it is all in your perspective, in your choice of thoughts. If you listen and pay attention to your body, it will tell you your thoughts are hurting it. Breathe deeply. Focus your gaze on something of beauty. Know how incredibly loved you are. Forgive yourself, and forgive those around you. Don't spend your precious thought time contemplating another's weakness. Dismiss the thought as quickly as it comes.

Play

Play is one of the most important activities you can engage in. It's good for your body, soul, and mind. We spend so much time, energy, and money on eating and exercising, when all we really need to do is follow our instincts for what sounds fun and makes us laugh. If you do this, the whimsical, carefree land of your childhood will sprinkle you with pixie dust. Your blood pressure and stress level will go down. Find creative ways to play every day. Be deliberate. Life is meant to be fun, not a long, monotonous car ride. Use your imagination. Tell stories. Dance in the kitchen. Wish on a star. Tell a funny joke. Laugh at yourself.

Nature

S pend as much time as you can in nature each day for physical, emotional, and spiritual rejuvenation. Have healthy, vibrant plants inside and outside your home. When you are spending time in nature, take several deep, delicious breaths and continually say "thank you" to God for this masterful creation. Have simple practices in your life that honor nature. Refill your own drinking bottle instead of buying plastic ones. Bring your own shopping bag to the store. Drive less and bike or walk more. Recycle everything you can. Even if you find a plastic bottle someone threw on the ground, pick it up and recycle it. As you do each small act of kindness toward the preservation of your planet, do it with great love and appreciation toward Mother Earth. Thoughts are everything. If 7 billion people shifted their consciousness around nature, things would change overnight.

We Are One

Be kind and loving toward every other person on the planet because we are all one. Literally when you hurt another, you hurt yourself. When you show love and kindness to another, you are treating yourself with love. Even if someone is rude or hurtful, continue to be kind and loving. Your example will help them remember their own true nature, which is also loving-kindness. This might not happen right away. Be patient. See the very best in everyone around you. Picture your kids cooperating and helping each other. Imagine a marriage that is tender and intimate. Visualize yourself doing work that is invigorating and abundant. Spend a few minutes playing these scenarios out. Watch them over and over until you are watching with your physical eyes.

Vibration

Every person and every thing has a vibration. There is nothing more important than keeping your vibration positive. Most people never think about their own vibration. People will spend large amounts of money on their physical appearance, clothing, and automobiles in an effort to make a favorable impression on others. All you need to do to positively impact those around you is think loving thoughts of gratitude. Smile and look at another eye to eye. Acknowledge them. By showing up in each moment, fully present, and deciding to be God's light and love in the room, you will send your vibration through the roof. People are not truly impressed by fancy cars and clothing, they just want to feel good. Good vibrations are contagious. Manage your vibration and everything else will fall into place for you.

Dawn

(friend)

It doesn't have to be so hard. Be in the moment you are in with all your heart, loving completely. Be authentic. Be yourself. Listen more. Laugh more. Give away your essence, and it will be replenished immediately. See yourself as the magnificent spirit that you are. How you see yourself is everything. See yourself as healthy and fit, and your body will obey. See yourself as a loving, kind parent and spouse, and you will be. Spend time seeing yourself as you would like to be each day and you can't help but become this vision. Breathe deeply and enjoy the simple pleasures that surround you each day:

The smell of freshly baked bread

The sun shining on your back

The tight hug of a loved one

The cozy warmth of your dog sleeping on your lap

The soft, white sand on your feet as you walk along the beach

The stars and moon in all their splendor on a clear night

Notice and appreciate each and every one. Let this be your focus each day, and your life will be better than your wildest dreams.

Beauty

There is so much beauty everywhere you look. Notice it! People are walking around oblivious to the miraculous beauty surrounding them. Take off your blindfold. Notice the flowers blooming, the leaves changing, and the colors of the sunset. Look deep into the eyes of your beloved and notice that love. Wake up! There is a magnificent symphony performing for you each day, but you are wearing earplugs. As you wake up, speak out loud about the beauty you see. This will help those around you to wake up as well. The more you recognize and appreciate the beauty of life, the more beauty you will see, until all you see each day are the breathtaking miracles of God's creation.

Talking

Words are so powerful. Most of what we talk about is negative. If you chose to only think and use positive, uplifting words, your entire life would improve miraculously. Be comfortable with silence. Many profound breakthroughs happen just after a period of silence. Listen to the words you offer as if you were making a movie of your life. Even make directorial comments in your head about your choice of words in a given scene. There is something about getting outside of yourself that helps develop your own self-awareness. Send yourself positive words of appreciation every time you know you got it right. These good thoughts and feelings lead to more good choices, which create a positive loop. Start right now. Speak words of love and appreciation toward yourself and everyone in your life.

Death

Don't fear death. You go on. You are still connected. You can't be disconnected. Each of us will leave this planet at the precise moment we are meant to. People should focus on living each day, each moment the very best they can. People should love big, give big, laugh big. Then, when death comes, there will be no regrets, no missed opportunities. There will be a satisfying feeling of completion, of a job well done. Talk to your loved ones in Heaven. They hear every word. If you get very quiet in your head, you can hear them too. Love in your life as much as you can, and death will lose its power.

Children

One of the greatest gifts on Earth is children. Learn from your children how to lose yourself in the moment. They are clear about their needs and are good at expressing them. They don't spend time worrying about the future or regretting the past. There is only now, followed by another now, and still another. They find the fun, the play in each moment. The best thing you can ever do for your children is feel good in your life. Be God's light, love, joy, and peace manifested in this world. Only by being this living example can you help your children. Children don't learn from your words. They learn from your example. Talk less and follow your bliss, your own passion that lights you up. If you are struggling with this, just watch your children. They do it every time they play.

Passion

Have passion toward everything you do. Passion is like salt to food—without it, you can still eat the food, but it tastes bland. Passion comes from God. You come here full of passion. You can be just as passionate at 80 as 18. All the greats were full of passion, without exception. There are three things you can do to feel more passion. First, eat healthy, whole foods and drink lots of water so your body feels light. Second, be fully present in the moment. Third, notice the blessings all around you. If you do these three things, you will feel good physically and spiritually. Passion will naturally follow.

Be Here Now

Slow down. Notice everything around you. Notice what you smell. Is it coffee brewing? Fresh cut grass? What do you hear? Birds singing in the morning? The sound of the shower? The hum of the refrigerator? What do you feel in your body? A hollowness in your stomach telling you it's time to eat? A fluttery sensation in your solar plexus indicating some nervousness you may have? What do you see? Notice the beauty surrounding you—the blue of the sky next to the green grass on the hills. Pay attention to the colors in your life. Gaze upon the faces of your loved ones and let yourself dwell there for a while. When you eat, take your time to first appreciate the beauty of the food. Smell the delicious aroma. Savor each bite slowly and deliberately. Do these things and you will live a full, abundant life without regret

Give Love in Every Moment

(Dad)

In every moment of your life there is an opportunity to give love. Take the opportunity. Let your life be one long love song, with each beat, word, and rhythm standing out and yet flowing together. Even if you are doing something as mundane as folding clothes or pumping gas, flood your mind and soul with appreciative thoughts, and you will see God's miraculous love envelope every area of your life. Things you have been struggling with for years will easily fall into place. Seek opportunities to show love every day. Smile and say hello to the person passing you on the street. You came here first and foremost to love. Make it your number one priority every day.

Grandma Myrna

It goes so fast! Slow it down. Slow down the pace. Do less each day, but when you do something, do it consciously and with love. Smile more. Laugh more. Praise more. Encourage more. Hug more. Listen more. Pray more. Move more. But stress less. Eat less. Criticize less. Swear less. Judge less. Worry less. See everyone around you as God sees them. Nothing will change your life more. Focus on what you love about each person, and you will help that characteristic grow. Give no attention to negative situations. Train your mind to move back to what is lovely and beneficial in each moment. There are always two ways to look at a moment. Choose to see the gift in each moment, and your life will be blessed beyond anything you could have dreamed.

Follow Your Instincts

If you receive a creative idea or impulse that excites you, recognize that it is a gift from Heaven. Follow that impulse to the next step—and the next step after that. This is exactly how every great breakthrough has happened. It begins with one thought, one idea with a lot of excitement and passion around it. The next big thing could be right around the corner for you. Get really good at acting upon those ideas and impulses and God will take you places beyond any dream you have for your life. Ignore the doubting voice in your head that tells you your idea is unrealistic. Everything starts off being unrealistic until one person who can "see" what is not there brings it into reality. Take one small step at a time, but keep the momentum going around your idea. Spend a little time every day visualizing your idea as if it had already manifested. The speed of the manifestation will amaze and delight you.

Judgment

The difference between Heaven and Earth comes down to the thousands of choices you make each day. Make each decision, each word choice, each thought, and each action from a place of love. Try to see the situation from God's perspective. If you see a homeless person, a drug addict, or any other person you feel judgment toward, take a second, close your eyes, and picture that individual surrounded and enveloped in God's love. Remember, that person is God's special creation. God knows that person's potential. God has unconditional love for that person. God never gives up on any of us. When you see weakness in another, picture the person full of joy and peace. Ask God to bless this individual with abundance of every kind. This is the only way you can help others make real change.

Simple Things

The things that bring you the most joy and happiness are the simple things. It's not the fancy car or dream house. It's the homemade soup a friend brings you when you are sick. It's listening to the birds singing in the morning. It's the smell of freshly brewed coffee. It's the sun warming your back. It's the taste of a warm chocolate chip cookie dipped in cold milk. It's the feeling of clean sheets on your bed. It's the beauty of the sun setting or the night sky full of bright stars. It's candles and fresh flowers and soft music. It's the smell, sound, and sight of the ocean. It's the feeling you get when someone shares with you that you have inspired them, that you have made a positive impact on their life. It's knowing that you are enough, that God loves you exactly as you are.

Visualization is Everything

If you truly understood the power of your thought, you would spend less time "doing" and more time sitting quietly and "seeing" your life as you would like it to be. Once you have a clear picture and you play it over and over in your mind, it cannot not happen. You have built the car, filled it with gas, and hit the accelerator. Once the car begins to move, you will think, "but of course!" You knew it would go, and so it does. Get clear on what you want in your life. What kind of spouse/partner do you want? What is your dream job? What would your body look like if you had a magic wand? What would your bank account look like? What would your relationships be like? Your beliefs work in every area of your life. There is nothing too small or too big. You can see yourself running a marathon or ending world hunger. The power is in the picture—the movie you see in your mind. Make it detailed, clear, and vivid. God will do the rest.

Decide How Happy You Are Going To Be

Each person decides how happy he or she is going to be in each moment. Happiness and joy are choices you make. Once you learn how to get there, you can go there as often as you like. Study yourself. Don't be lazy in your thinking. What activities light you up? Hiking in a forest? Listening to classical music? Surfing? Coaching Little League? Cooking a gourmet meal? Planting a garden? Whatever it is, do it and do it often. Make the decision to be a joy-filled person. Smile often throughout your day, for no reason. Find things that make you laugh. Write love notes. Gifts warm your own heart as much as they do the receiver. When you decide to be happy and feel good, you will be showered with all kinds of reasons to be happy.

Thoughts Create Your Life

Today, pay attention to your thoughts. Most people never even notice the constant chatter in their own heads. People don't realize the power of this chatter. If they did, they would be much more disciplined and selective about the thoughts they think. One way you can tell whether the thoughts you are thinking are positive or negative is by the way you feel. If you feel sad or depressed, your constant mental chatter has to be negative. If you feel jubilant, eager or playful, your mental chatter is positive. You have control over the thoughts you think. Practice catching yourself thinking a negative thought and then soften the thought. If it is a thought of judgment toward someone, immediately think of something positive about the person. Flood your mind with gratitude and watch your life transform before your eyes.

Say Thank You

Say thank you as many times as possible every day. Say it out loud and in your head. Every time someone shows you kindness say thank you. Every time you see something beautiful or moving say thank you. Wear these words out. Let them linger in your mind like the screen saver on your laptop, ready to pop up at any moment. Let these words be the background music of your life. Send thank you cards, thank you emails, and thank you texts every day. When you are constantly saying thank you, there is no space for any negativity to creep into your head. You can't feel sorry for yourself or judge others when "thank you" is filling your headspace. Record in a journal each day those moments in which you are most thankful. This will profoundly improve your life.

Love

(Dad)

All day long, your job is to love. It doesn't matter if you are a CEO or stay-at-home parent. Find ways to love others all day, every day. Your life is a love song to God. Each word, thought, and action you choose is the unique expression of your love song. You don't have to try so hard. God will put the next part of the melody in your head, and all you have to do is follow your instincts and impulses. God will whisper in your ear. The more love you give, the more will come back, and a miraculous, powerful cycle will begin. Wake up in the morning looking for opportunities to show your love to anyone your life touches. It's why you came.

You Are the Creator of Your Life

(Dawn)

God put the paintbrush in your hand the day you were born. That is why children are so free to paint, draw, and mold their art. Each moment of your life is an opportunity to create something beautiful. It is your chance to follow your intuition and create something new and unique. Each moment is an opportunity to show kindness and love. Spend time dreaming about your life each day. What does the dream look like? Where are you? What does your house look like? What do you feel like in the dream? Who are you with? What do you look like? What are you wearing? Dreams tell you a lot about your innermost desires. God wouldn't give you a dream without a way to achieve it.

Your Job

Many people are unsure which job to choose or wonder if they are in the wrong job. You only have one job: to be as full of love and positivity as you can be in each moment. From this starting point, the perfect job, the perfect thing to say, the perfect inspired idea, and the perfect timing will flow naturally to you. Not only that, but when you are aligned with the most powerful force in the universe, you will expend less effort and achieve results way beyond your expectations. Start your day, each day, from a place of love and appreciation for everything in your life, from the soft pillow on your bed, to the perfectly brewed warm cup of coffee in your hand, to the sun rising every morning. If you are in a job you don't like, find what you do like about that job and say thank you. The more you do this, the more you will like about your job. Or you will be inspired to find a new job, but it won't be because you hate your current job. The love for the new job will propel you toward it.

Let Go

Without realizing it, many of us choose to walk through this life with a 50-pound backpack full of stress, worry, and judgment. Every time you think a thought that feels bad in any way, you are adding to the weight of the backpack. Pay attention to the thoughts you are thinking all day every day and start to change them. This will be difficult at first because you may be shocked at how many negative thoughts you think in a day. But as you develop your skill of flipping a negative thought into a positive one, you will begin to notice how much lighter and happier you feel. Imagine yourself tossing big, heavy pots and pans out of your pack. You are in control of the weight of your backpack, or whether you wear a pack at all.

Catch It

The moment you realize you are engaged in a negative, uncomfortable conversation, find a way to change the momentum. Sometimes it's simply saying out loud, "This conversation is too negative, let's talk about something more positive." Sometimes you can simply change the topic. Sometimes you need to excuse yourself. The important thing is to catch it the moment it is happening. Notice how you feel when negative momentum is building. Develop your skill of protecting your own positive energy. The more you do this, the easier and more natural it will become. People will stop bringing their negative energy to you because you will snuff it out from lack of oxygen.

Take Your Weather Wherever You Go

You create your own weather and take it with you wherever you go. What kind of weather have you created? Is it hot and humid where people have a hard time breathing around you? Is it sunny and clear? Is it stormy with thunder and lightning? Although you go through changes in your moods, your overall weather pattern is very important to your overall happiness. You can change your weather pattern, but you first have to realize that you are creating the weather around you. You have the pen in your hand, and you can write your story however you want it to be. If you want people to feel optimistic and uplifted in your presence, write that. If you want to bring out the best in everyone around you, write that. If you want people to leave your presence feeling better about themselves, write that. If you want your life to be one miracle or blessing after the next, write that. That is exactly what will happen.

Your Body

We spend so much time thinking about our bodies, and most of the time they're negative, condemning thoughts. Your body is a beautiful, miraculous creation of God. The only thoughts you should ever think about your body are "thank you" thoughts. "Thank you for carrying me around wherever I want to go, all day, every day. " "Thank you for finding a way to process it when I eat too much or sleep too little." "Thank you for sending me signals and warning signs even though I often ignore them. You never give up." Find things you love and appreciate about your body and focus on these attributes. Think of your body as a loyal, non-complaining employee that shows up day after day, doing his or her job, even with your constant verbal and physical criticism. Your body hears every thought you think. Think some good thoughts about this magnificent vessel God blessed you with.

Joy

You came here to experience joy. You came to laugh and smile and play. You came to be so immersed in the joy of the moment that you forget yourself. You came to follow your inspired ideas. You came to do what sounded like the most fun in each moment. You came to share these moments with the ones you love. You came to receive blessings everywhere you turn: a sunset that leaves you speechless, a meadow after a sparkling rain, twinkling stars in a black sky. You came to be full of love, laughter, and appreciation for this world and everyone in it. The question is, are you doing what you came to do?

Train Your Brain to See the Good

You can train your brain to see the good or the best in every moment of your life. Trust that God has a much better perspective or vantage point than you do. What may seem to you to be a roadblock or dead-end, may just be God's way of leading you to an ever better, more fulfilling life. But in order to receive the full blessings bestowed upon you, you must be thankful and have faith that everything always works out. No matter where you are in your life, God is ready to lead you to higher ground. But you must voluntarily follow God's gentle whispers. You must be thankful for where you are right now. Be thankful for the body you are in right now. Be thankful for the relationship you are in right now. Be thankful for the moment you are in right now. Only from this place of gratitude can God lead you to higher ground.

Bless and Be Blessed

We have so much extra "thought time" we waste with negative thoughts. Train yourself to spend this extra thought time blessing everyone in your life. Ask for a blessing upon every person on your street, in your city, in your state, in your country, and in the world. When you are at a sporting event, ask for a blessing upon every player on both teams, the parents and fans, the coaches, and the referees. Bless the checker at the grocery store and everyone in line. Bless your employees, customers, and suppliers. Bless your kids' teachers, coaches, and friends. See all of the people in your life surrounded by the white light of God's love. See them happy and joyful, living a life of abundance. As you send out all of these blessings, you will experience a profound shift in your own life.

Making Your Dreams Your Reality

Whatever you dream about, you can bring into your life. God doesn't give us unattainable dreams. The more good feelings you derive from your dreams, the more you know they are meant to be in your reality. Spend time in your dream world everyday. This is not wasted time, but rather very powerful work. Be as detailed in your dream as you can be. Notice the smells, the sounds, and the feelings of your dream world. If you begin to focus on something less pleasing or annoying, get out of the dream immediately. You are in a very powerful captain's chair, and you don't want to steer the ship toward an iceberg.

Follow Your Excitement

(Dawn)

Follow the breadcrumbs of whatever excites you. If you see a recipe that sounds delicious, make it. If the idea pops in your head to make a dinner for a friend going through a tough time, do it. If you read about a place that you would love to visit, plan a trip. If someone tells you about a fabulous book, movie, or restaurant, try it. Variety is good for you. Get out of your rut. Switch it up. Pay attention to what lights you up. That is your path. You don't have to worry about where the path will lead. If you are enjoying the journey on the path, you are doing what you came to do. Get really good at following your excitement in each moment, and your life will be the very best life you could ever imagine.

If It Feels Bad, Turn Away

If you notice you are thinking thoughts that make you feel bad, focus your mind on thoughts of gratitude and appreciation. Choose any thought that makes you feel better, and keep your focus on these good feeling thoughts. Maybe you think of a funny memory. Maybe you focus on someone you love and all of their positive characteristics. Maybe you put on some good music or take a run or a hot bath. Maybe you go for a hike in nature or meditate quietly. Find things that will distract you from the negative thoughts and feelings. Take one baby step at a time.

Picture Yourself in Heaven

Imagine taking your last breath and then watching your entire life movie from Heaven. Can you see that your soul in Heaven would see every single scene through the eyes of unconditional love? From Heaven, you would see that in each moment you choose a light thought or a dark thought, and that thought leads to another, and another. You would see the power of the first thought. You would realize that your thoughts create your life and your level of happiness. From Heaven, you would see the importance of slowing down, doing less, and just "being." You would realize the importance of stressing less and playing more. If you could do it over, you would give and love and hug and dance and laugh and smile all day long. You would live Heaven on Earth!

The Part and the Whole

We are each the part and the whole. The whole exists within each of us, and each of us is an essential part of the whole. Be yourself. Trust yourself. That little voice is God whispering. Be still enough to hear it. God doesn't want you to sit in a dark room waiting to hear His voice. God wants you to sing and dance and hike and eat and work and play. God will come through when you are fully engaged, enjoying and appreciating all of the gifts of the world. You will receive a sign at the perfect time. God and your angels are saying, "Yes! That's it!" Pay attention to the thought you had right before you received the sign. Be open. Be light. Be fun. Be playful. Be love. Be present.

I Am

I am God's love in this world. I am peace. I am fun. I am a blessing. I am a gift. I am joy. I am wisdom. I am truth. I am nature. I am present. I am the creator of my story. I am the captain of my ship. I am the dreamer of the dream. I am pure. I am lovely. I am beauty. I am unconditional love. I am connected to all other living beings. I am gratitude. I am light. I am love. I am luminescent. I am an uplifter. I am a light worker. I am calm. I am easy about things. I am trust. I am doing what I came here to do.

Less is More

Do less. Talk less. Complain less. Worry less. Feel more. Love more. Hug more. Laugh more. Dance more. Play more. Savor more. Pray more. Write more. Say "thank you" more. Dream more. Travel more. Meditate more. Nap more. Smile more. Make love more. Think good thoughts more. Spend time with uplifting people more. Relax more. Listen to your inner voice more.

Do Your Thing

Everyone has a passion. You came to experience that passion. When you are living your passion, you ignite the passion in those around you. Whenever you get the opportunity to experience your passion, take it. That lit-up feeling you get is your indicator that you are doing the right thing. Time takes on a different dimension. Time passes extremely fast, and yet you don't feel rushed. You feel great in your body. You are confidant and focused, but at the same time you forget about yourself because you are so engrossed in the moment. Inspiration and creative ideas flow easily and effortlessly. Start moving toward that which you find exciting and interesting. Your passion is waiting for you.

Be Yourself

You are such a gift to this world. You have no idea how much the world needs exactly what you have to offer. Right now, today, there is somebody waiting for you to get aligned with God and receive the inspiration for your next thought, word, or action. Every thought you are thinking affects those around you. If you understood how incredibly important you are to the whole world, you would make your life's work to line up with God and then listen for the whispers. Your life is supposed to be fun, joyous, interesting, and worthwhile. When you are your true self, you forget yourself. You become the part of you that is divine. You see people and things through the eyes of God. This is your gift to yourself and to the world.

Each Day

When you wake up each morning, write down words that inspire you: words like fun, laughter, peace, calm, ease, joy, smile, love, create, feel, savor, light, breathe, clarity, synchronicity, inspiration, present, gratitude, appreciation. Write any words that come to you, that feel good. Set your intention for the day first thing in the morning. By simply writing down these guiding words in the morning, you will bring them into your life that day. Better yet, write these words on notecards and place them where you will see them throughout your day. Watch the power of these words begin to powerfully shape your life.

When the Horse Throws You Off, Get Back On

Sometimes things happen in life that knock you to your knees. When this happens, don't beat yourself up thinking you weren't strong enough to stay on the horse. If you find yourself in a negative vibration, take a nap or meditate. The moment you wake up, begin thinking thoughts of love and gratitude. Start small. "I love my warm, cozy bed." "The birds sound lovely singing outside my window." "I really like Sharon in Accounting. She is always so helpful and positive." Write down more things for which you feel strong appreciation—family members, close friends, pets, etc. Think thoughts of gratitude toward your body, your financial situation, the food you will eat that day, your car, anything that touches your life. Send a text to someone you love and let them know how much you appreciate them. Show them by your actions. Flood your thoughts with love and appreciation for everything in your life. Before you know it, you will be back on the horse and jumping hurdles.

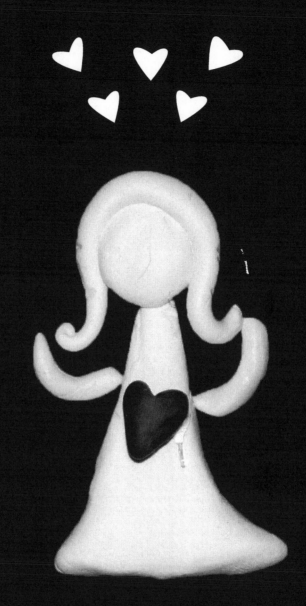

PART 3 | RIGHT HANDED NUGGETS

The following Nuggets were written with my dominant right hand. When I walk or hike alone in nature, a voice from Heaven comes through fairly often. It's like I'm listening to a Ted Talk specifically about whatever is happening in my life at that moment. As soon as I get home, I start writing so that I don't forget the message. I pray these Nuggets bless you as well.

Hearing God's Voice

The weeks and months that followed my dad's transition to Heaven were indescribably difficult for my stepmother, Gloria. They did everything together. They spent hours talking and walking. Other than their kids and grandkids, they spent the majority of their time with each other. Just recently Gloria shared with me how angry she was at my dad for leaving her. My dad had a plan to set Gloria up financially prior to his death. Together they purchased 10 rental homes. No one could foresee the real estate crash of 2009. Gloria ended up in a huge financial nightmare, resulting in the foreclosure of three of their homes. But the financial stress came nowhere near the emotional pain and loneliness that enveloped her.

In October 2009, about four months after my dad died, Gloria had an experience that would change the course of her life. The day started out like any other day. Gloria took her long morning walk in beautiful sunny San Diego. But as she walked, she started to feel sick to her stomach and dizzy. When she finally arrived back home, she proceeded to throw up in the bathroom for two hours. It was in the bathroom that she heard the clear, calm, objective voice of God. One sentence: "You can go now if you want to." It was very matter of fact. Her immediate response was, "No, I want to stay and learn what I need to learn." That was it. She was given an out, and she refused. Her true spiritual journey came out of a desire to stay connected to her beloved Bud. She read every book she could find on the journey beyond this life. From this point, she opened herself to many different spiritual topics from feng shui to the power of crystals and everything in between. She and I stay connected through a daily telephone conversation in which we share our "God stories." We read the same books and listen to the same YouTube videos. Our relationship has moved to an entirely new level since June of 2009. Although I was always close to my dad and Gloria, we never talked about spiritual things. Now it is our lifeline to my dad.

In the last year, through "coincidences" (which I don't believe in), Gloria was led to a spiritual church in San Diego. This church focuses on healings and communicating messages from our angels and spirits that have passed over. Gloria has completed the necessary classes to become a certified healer in the church. She has been told on many occasions that the love flowing out of her is palpable. She is often the "battery" by which the angels and spirits are able to come through and give messages to those present. Gloria spends an hour praying out loud each morning. I feel such peace when she is praying for my family members and me. Although Gloria still has her challenges, the joy and growth she is experiencing as a soul are remarkable to watch. She recently shared with me this epiphany: Had my dad not gone to Heaven when he did, she would not have experienced this profound spiritual growth. The Nugget she and I received when she heard God's voice was that even our most painful, challenging experiences come with great blessings. Just because we are in extraordinary pain does not mean God has abandoned us. Quite the opposite. It's in these raw, jagged periods in our lives that we are open to God's wisdom, grace, and miracles. When we transform these valleys of our lives into healing, growth opportunities, we ascend to the top of the mountain and see the view like never before.

Signs From Above

When my dad went to Heaven, I received several signs that gave me incredible comfort. One of the reasons I believe he was able to come through to me was because rather than being stricken with grief, I very quickly was blessed with the understanding that this was how it was supposed to be. Although I was in shock, I quickly got over the "poor me" state and moved into the "how can I stay connected to my dad" state.

Although I could list many, many signs I've received, a few stand out in particular. My first trip back to my dad's home in San Diego with my kids was a little scary. I wasn't sure how any of us would handle it. But like everything else on this journey, I just moved forward and figured I would have lots of help getting through it. I asked my dad for a sign before the trip. Somehow I felt if we got a sign from him, it would make the bittersweet experience of staying in his home more comforting. I sure got my sign. We literally pulled into his garage, started pulling our suitcases out of the car when an earthquake started rolling the car back and forth. You would think I would have immediately recognized this as a sign from my dad, but it actually took me a few days to connect the dots. I've noticed this is often the case. Our very powerful, "thinking" minds can block our intuitive "knowing" minds.

A second sign I received was one that I immediately recognized as a gift from my dad, particularly because there was no other explanation. My oldest son, Cameron, and I were in the kitchen. The heavy, red rubber kitchen mitt flopped from the kitchen counter into the sink all by itself! I said out loud, "We love you too Dad!"

The day my Aunt Bobbi died in 2014, an unusual red dragonfly showed up in my backyard. It flew around my yard for an entire day. I even took a picture of it and texted it to my cousin Debbi. I told her I thought it was a sign from her mom. The following day the dragonfly disappeared. I had yet to speak to my cousin on the phone since her mom had died. We both knew it would be a difficult conversation and we would both break down. But it had been a week since my aunt's passing, and I knew we needed to face this. The second I dialed my cousin's number and headed out to the backyard, the red dragonfly reappeared! My cousin and I both felt a strange peace that my aunt was watching over us.

The best way to receive a sign is to ask for one. Let it go. Watch what shows up. Spirits are very creative and sometimes clever. One time I wanted a sign from my dad, so I got very quiet and just waited to see what would come. The first image I got was of Superman. I found this funny because when my son Cameron was little, he played with some superhero dolls that my dad and Gloria bought for him. He would always assign the role of Superman to my dad. I can also remember my dad and Gloria dressing up for a Halloween party one year. He was Superman and she was Wonder Woman. I waited several weeks after I asked for the sign but never saw Superman anywhere. I finally forgot about my request. A few weeks later I was sitting outside at a restaurant in Las Vegas with Gloria and my three kids. I was overtaken with emotion when a man dressed in a full Superman costume walked right by our table. I loved that my Dad waited until we were with Gloria to give us his sign.

Momentum

We can't discuss vibration without also discussing momentum. Esther Hicks says in the book Ask and it is Given that it takes 17 seconds to establish momentum, good or bad. The sooner we can identify the momentum we have going, the sooner we can add to it or change it. Most of us are completely unaware of our ability to create momentum. When we notice how we feel in a particular moment, that is our indication of what kind of momentum we have created. Imagine you join a group of your friends who are discussing a very negative topic. Notice how this makes you feel in your body. Most of us just join in the conversation. We have now started negative momentum. If someone brings up a topic that makes you feel bad, excuse yourself or change the topic as quickly as possible. Most of the thoughts we think each day repeat themselves the next day, and the next. That is why it is so important to stop those negative thoughts immediately. Your thoughts create your life. Notice how a song, television show, movie, or website makes you feel. Grocery stores play sad love songs from 20 years ago. Have you ever noticed how you feel in the grocery store? Don't get hooked. Guard your vibration and notice as soon as negative momentum starts.

Learn how to create your own positive momentum and keep it going for as long as you can. Do what you love everyday. If you love to hike, hike as much as you can. Fill your thoughts with the beauty of nature. Think about how blessed you are to have your family and friends. Say thank you that you are able to do the work you do. The more time you spend thinking thoughts of gratitude for every blessing in your life, the longer you will keep positive momentum going. Artists, inventors, and writers understand the power of momentum. They have harnessed momentum to create. We can all do this. It's simply a skill that takes practice.

One way to start your day with positive momentum is to begin a writing practice first thing in the morning. When I get up in the morning one of the first things I do is set the timer on the oven for 11 minutes. I write my gratitude list, prayer list, and dream list. Setting a timer helps me keep the pen on the paper the entire time. This is the most important work I do each day. I am creating my life on the pages of my journal. Even if you are a reluctant writer, start by doodling the words "thank you" on a scratch piece of paper. There is something powerful in the written word. The next week add one specific item for which you are grateful. It could be a moment from the previous day. The key is the emotion you feel around this thought. Emotion is what drives momentum. If you learn how to manufacture positive emotion, you are on your way to the life of your dreams. In each moment of your life, ask yourself "What could I do or think to feel my very best in this moment?" Sometimes the answer could be to take a nap, bath, or walk. Sometimes we simply need to reframe the way we are looking at a particular situation. When we focus on the blessings in each situation, we rev up our positive momentum. It's easier to stop negative momentum right away, before it gets real speed. Disease is negative momentum that has gone unchecked. If you are feeling anger or frustration, it's best to deal with it honestly and head on. Then get back to your good feeling state.

Nugget #4

Focus on the Blessings

There are two ways to view every situation in your life. You can view situations as curses or blessings. Even what might be viewed as a very negative situation has blessings. The sooner we start focusing on the blessings in a situation, the sooner we begin receiving more blessings. Whatever we focus on we get more of. When my Dad died, I received many blessings right away. My Dad despised illness and hospitals. Dying in his sleep was a huge blessing. Gloria was with family that loved her. He lived a wonderful life that he felt good about. Since his death, Gloria has grown tenfold spiritually, as have I. I feel my Dad helping us constantly, rooting us on.

Another example of looking for the good is illustrated through the story of a little nine-year-old girl named Breezy, one of my daughter's best friends. When Breezy discovered she had a very aggressive form of cancer in her left knee, she had a difficult decision to make. Rather than risk the cancer spreading, Breezy bravely faced having her left leg amputated. Rather than focusing on her loss, Breezy and her family focused on their blessings. They still have their daughter. They received so much love and support on this journey. I remember Breezy's mom telling me she wouldn't have been surprised if the surgeons amputating Breezy's leg actually lifted up off the ground during the surgery. She said you could actually feel all of the prayers coming through from all over the world in that moment. Breezy and her siblings received stunning room makeovers through an organization called Rooms of Hope. She also received a running leg from Challenged Athlete Foundation. But the greatest blessing Breezy and her family have received on this journey has been the opportunity to help other families. Breezy often meets with kids who have been diagnosed with cancer to show them not only her leg but, more importantly, her bright, shining spirit.

Have you ever noticed how some people who have had an incredibly challenging story rise to the highest heights? We can take what happens to us in life and channel it, transform it into fuel for positive momentum. We are all capable of so much more than we realize. When we focus on the blessings we already have, we can create anything we want in our lives.

Nugget #5

Meditation

When you hear the word meditation, how does it make you feel? For many people, the idea of sitting with a blank mind for extended periods of time sounds torturous. The health benefits of meditation have been very well documented and are now accepted by the medical community. Meditation reduces stress, lowers blood pressure, and strengthens the immune system. Meditation brings you into the present moment. We spend so much time worrying about the future or regretting the past, when our lives are happening right now, in this moment. The only way we can fully embrace our lives is if we are consciously living in this moment. There are so many different ways to meditate. It doesn't matter which one you choose, just that you do it consistently—preferably every day.

One of the simplest meditations is a simple breathing exercise that you can do any time, anywhere. Focusing on our breath immediately connects us to our bodies and the present moment.

Dr. Andrew Weil offers this simple meditation in his CD series, The Spontaneous Happiness Prescription.

Exhale completely.

Inhale for a count of 4.

Hold for a count of 7.

Exhale for a count of 8.

Repeat this sequence 4 times. When you do this meditation practice regularly, you will find your body immediately relaxes.

I have several meditation compact discs. Each day I choose one depending on how much time I have and my needs. If I only have 15 minutes, I may choose a binaural beats meditation from YouTube or a 15-minute Abraham Hicks meditation. I love the Oprah/Deepak Chopra 21-day meditation challenges as well. You can lie down, sit upright, or even walk as you meditate. The most important element is that you connect with your breath and body and rest the busy ego part of your brain. When I walk the path around my house in the morning, I often receive "downloads" from God and my angels. These are thoughts and ideas that come to me spontaneously. When we are in a meditative state, we are open to receive information—or Nuggets—from Heaven.

Fun!

My Aunt Bobbi lost her battle to colon cancer a few years ago. I remember watching the tears run down her cheeks as my cousin Debbi and I massaged her feet as she received chemo. She was so sad to be leaving her husband of 50 years, my Uncle Jim. She adored her three girls and seven grandchildren. We all prayed for a miracle, but it was her time. After she went home, I asked Barbara, a pychic in San Diego, to connect with my Aunt Bobbi in Heaven. Barbara said my Aunt Bobbi realized how it is supposed to be fun here on Earth. We are supposed to enjoy this journey. We make it much more painful and stressful than it needs to be. We stress over things we should lift up and let be. God made the Earth incredibly beautiful and fun, just for our enjoyment. Are you enjoying this gift? How often do you get out in nature and soak up the good energy? Do you play in the ocean waves? They aren't just for the dolphins and seals. Do you build snowmen? Engage in a playful snowball fight? Ski? Just picturing the mountains covered in snow makes me feel warm and cozy. There is so much natural beauty and fun to be had on this planet, but we have to train ourselves to make it part of our lives. Somehow we have decided we will work 51 weeks of the year so that we can take one week off to have fun when we are on vacation. Fun should be part of every day of our lives. Recently I took my daughter and a few of her friends to San Francisco to ice skate in an open rink. She wanted to know if I would skate with her. After saying no three times, I finally acquiesced. And I'm so glad I did! It was a complete blast. I started wondering why my knee-jerk reaction was to say no. A friend broke her ankle ice skating a few years before, and I realized fear was behind my hesitation.

We also put off fun because we decide we are too busy. But fun can take place anywhere at any time. Whether we dance in the kitchen while making dinner or sing at the top of our lungs in the carpool, we can choose to sprinkle every day with fun.

God is fun and funny. When we are light, easy, and fun, God and our angels can come through to us more easily. The more we let ourselves be guided by these higher beings, the more serendipity, joy, and fun we will have on our journey. When we realize our time here is quite short, it makes sense that we should have as much fun as possible, enjoying simple pleasures every day and loving everyone God places in our path.

Nugget #7

Choosing from the Thought Buffet

People don't realize the power of their thoughts. Our thoughts create our lives. If you are unhappy with some part of your life, perhaps taking a good hard look at your own mental chatter could be the beginning of the solution. Imagine you are at a huge food buffet with hundreds of dishes. Everything from perfectly grilled salmon to warm, gooey, homemade chocolate chip cookies are being served. When you choose to worry or complain (out loud or in your head,) it is like you are choosing a big, slimy, green plate of moldy mush. It tastes bad in your mouth, gives you indigestion, if not nausea, and, if consumed regularly, could make you chronically ill. If a negative, unproductive thought enters your mind, just politely put it back on the buffet table. Choose a healthier, more nutritious option that nourishes your body and soul. No need to beat yourself up—this too is like taking more of the mush. The sooner you can start savoring the scrumptious taste of warm, pecan pie a la mode or a perfectly sun-ripened caprese salad, the sooner your life will start falling into place.

The Purpose of Our Bodies

God put this really cool internal device in each of our bodies called hunger. When we feel it, we should eat, not to the point of discomfort but to the point of satisfaction. Have you ever noticed there are no obese animals in nature? They instinctively know how much their bodies need. We do too. Eating is one of the great pleasures of living. Many people have an unhealthy relationship with their bodies. Our bodies are simply the vehicles God lends us for this journey. At the end of our lives, we turn our vehicle back into God. The purpose of our bodies is to provide us pleasure while we love everyone God places in our path. Period. The more we appreciate and nurture our bodies, the more they naturally transform into their ideal state. Your body's ideal state may be different than your ego's. Go with the former, you will be much happier. It isn't our job to question why we are 5'2" or have red hair. Our job is to do the best with what we have been given. So thank your body right now. Thank your feet for all of the pounding they take. Thank your legs for transporting you everywhere you want to go. Thank your torso and all of its amazing organs that we all take for granted. Thank your arms for carrying your loads. Thank your head for seeing, smelling, tasting, and hearing. Thank your heart for all of the love it emanates to everyone you touch. Do this every day, either silently or, better yet, out loud, and watch the transformation that happens from the inside out.

Breathe In, Breath Out

Many people walk around breathing in pollution (negative thoughts) completely unaware of the impact these thoughts have on their lives. When we think a loving, grateful thought and feel the feeling that accompanies that thought, we rise up, just a little, out of the smog. We pet our dogs and linger over the warmth and comfort their furry bodies bring to the moment. Breathe in, breathe out, move up. We hug our beloved and hold the embrace a few extra seconds as we silently think, "Thank you for being in my life." Breathe in, breathe out, move up. We wake up a little earlier than usual. We light a candle and write in a gratitude journal, thanking God for each gift in our lives, big and small. Breathe in, breathe out, move up. We take a walk in nature and notice the magnificence, from the green, lush trees to the dew sparkling on the grass. Breathe in, breathe out, move up. We make a meal for a friend in pain. We say a prayer that the food will help heal her body and soul. Breathe in, breathe out, move up. We notice the sun is shining above the smog. The sky is blue and clear. We like how this feels. Breathe in, breathe out, move up.

Nugget #10

Jump in the Water!

When you feel excited about a certain endeavor in your life, jump in with a cannonball splash! I have been dabbling in all kinds of inspirational projects for the past few years. I put some work and energy into their manifestation but not enough for them to really take off. It's fine to have temporary hobbies and projects, but my heart was longing to write this book and share my gift. I needed to jump in, immerse myself, and hold my breath for a bit. This is the scary part. The shock of the water temperature can be uncomfortable until your body adjusts. I would talk myself out of jumping in for all sorts of reasons. But finally I got to the point where staring longingly at the water, imagining how fun and invigorating it would be, was more painful than overcoming my fear and just going for it. I know God and my angels will be right by my side the whole journey, so there is nothing to fear. Sometimes we just have to have a little faith and push ourselves off the cliff in order to experience the true bliss of living our dream. So here I gooooooo!

Nugget #11

Inner Soul

In my Nuggets From Heaven seminar, I pass out a puzzle piece to each attendee and then ask, "Who has the most important piece?" Everyone looks at his own puzzle piece carefully. After inspecting the puzzle pieces, one brave soul says, "They are all important." Ding Ding Ding! Of course they are. We are each a puzzle piece, essential to the completion of the puzzle. We are equally important but unique. We have to be authentically ourselves to "click in" to our place in the puzzle. When we do what truly lights us up in each moment of our lives, we are listening to our inner soul. It is then that God and our angels can work through us. When we think loving, appreciative thoughts toward ourselves and everyone around us, God's spirit is strong in us. Life begins to transform into one miraculous experience after another. We are in flow.

In the children's book, You Are Special, by Max Lucado, a toy-maker creates a wooden boy who is labeled with stickers by every-one in the town. When he does something good, he receives a gold star sticker. When he does something undesirable, he receives a gray circle sticker. Unfortunately this little boy is covered in gray circle stickers. One day he meets a girl who hasn't any stickers. He asks her how that can be. She tells him she visits the toymaker every day. The boy immediately sets off to visit the toymaker, who explains that he is perfect in his eyes. He tells him "I am your creator. You are perfect exactly as you are." The boy learns that if he cares only about the opinion of his creator, and not of the other toys, the stickers will not stick to him. As he leaves the toymaker's shop, the first gray sticker falls off.

When we connect with our inner soul and tap into the divine connection we each have, we get out of the ego, out of our heads, and into our true spirit. Whenever we are thinking a thought of lack, judgment, or fear, we are not connecting with our inner spirit. Here is a simple acronym I use to remember how to connect with my spirit: BMW.

B stands for breath and bubbles. Whenever you take a deep breath, you connect to your soul. Our breath connects our soul to our bodies. Taking several deep, full belly breaths always centers and grounds me. B also stands for bubbles. Whenever I am wor-rying about someone or frustrated by someone, I picture the little girl in my canvas work surrounded by heart-shaped bubbles. I pic-ture her sending those love bubbles to the person in pain. I see the hearts gently popping all of over the person, filling them with love and peace. What's interesting about this technique is that it always brings me so much peace. It immediately changes my energy from negative to positive.

M stands for moment. The only way to connect with your soul is in the present moment. If you are thinking about the past or the future, you are not fully engaged in the now. Notice everything around you. Notice the colors you see. Notice the sounds you hear. Notice the smells. Notice how you feel. Notice everything in your physical experience. Say thank you silently or out loud.

W stands for wave. Every thought we think, every word, every action reverberates as a wave out into the universe. We literally change the world around us when we change our thoughts and actions. A prayer, blessing, or thought of gratitude changes the world in a spiritual and physical way. There is nothing that doesn't count. Just like Gandhi said, "Be the change that you want to see in the world."

Power of Prayer

Praying actually changes the physical world we live in. A prayer is a manifestation. When we pray, we create an intention, a vision, a dream. If we pray with faith, we let go of the prayer as soon as we send it out into the universe, trusting that God will do what is best in each situation. The more time we spend "seeing" the outcome we desire, the more power our prayer has. This is why we should never worry or spend time creating negative experiences in our minds. We can create these too. There is nothing too small to lift up to God in prayer. God and our angels care about everything we care about. When we make a request, we harness the power of God and our angels to move mountains. The more faith we have, the more powerful our prayers. The next time you are worried or stressed about something, picture the issue in your hands, then extend your hands up over your head and ask God to take this worry from you. I have had so many sleepless nights worrying about various issues, usually pertaining to my children. Exhausted, I would finally lift up the worry and immediately receive God's peace. I would always wonder why I didn't do that first. Train yourself to go to God in prayer first. It's a discipline, a habit, like any other productive habit in your life. You will see and experience miracles that are only explainable by God's grace.

Nugget #13

Spiritual Health

One definition of health is a body strong enough to maintain equilibrium when outside pressures are applied. The same is true for your emotional and spiritual health. One morning I got up early to go on my favorite hike. I was feeling great, enjoying the beauty of trees, flowers, and birds. I was focused on how blessed I am to live in such a gorgeous place with so many fantastic hikes within 10 minutes of my home.

Before I began my hike, I stopped by the public restroom, which was locked. I walked to the closest café, and even though the place was empty, the owner told me I couldn't use his restroom since it was for paying customers only. No wonder the place was empty. I then walked to the nearest grocery store. After using the restroom, I found some darling paper plates on sale for $1.49. They weren't marked, and when I told the checker the price, she said "There is no way these are $1.49, since the napkins are $5.99." Her tone was quite rude and accusatory. When she verified the price I gave her, she mumbled an apology. I decided to send her love bubbles and told her to have a wonderful day. As I left the grocery store, I was curious about the negative experiences I was attracting. It was then that God gave me the answer. The strength of my vibration was being tested. I decided I was up for the challenge. I sent another big burst of love bubbles to both the café owner and the grocery store checker and headed up the mountain. As I was hiking, I asked my angels to give me my next nugget to write. In that moment, my whole morning experience came rushing back to me. I stopped at the top of the mountain to write this nugget in the notes section of my phone. Isn't it funny how you can always find the blessing in a situation if you truly look for it?

Nugget #14

Get To vs. Got To

We came here to do what lights us up in each moment. When we do this, God and our angels are able to use us to positively impact everyone else we touch. It's like we are bumper cars, and when we follow our bliss, our car is moving, interacting with all of the other cars. God can place our moving car exactly where it is needed most. When we are bored, stressed, worried, negative, or judgmental toward others, we are like the bumper car stuck in the corner, going nowhere. Even if there are activities you need to do each day that you are not particularly lit up about, you can change your attitude from "I've got to" to "I get to." Perhaps you don't like your current job. Wake up each morning and write a list of all of the positive elements of your job. Does your job pay your bills? Do you have a good friend or mentor you met at your job? By focusing on what you love and appreciate about your current job, you will naturally and easily attract an even better job.

Perhaps you are a mother or father and you spend a great deal of time shuttling your children to school, sports, and other activities. As you are driving, focus on being grateful that you have children. Be grateful that your children are able to go to school. Focus on how wonderful it is that your kids have activities that light them up and that you are able to show your love by supporting your children's activities.

Maybe you are facing a health challenge. What could your body be trying to tell you? Do you need to slow down? Maybe you have always been extremely self reliant and this current health situation is teaching you to accept help from others. Be thankful for the doctors and health care professionals helping you. Thank the on-line community that generously gives valuable advice and information. Send up prayers of gratitude for your family and friends supporting you unconditionally.

There are so many gifts and blessings in each moment of our lives. Be a blessing detective. Scour every situation for the obvious and not-so-obvious gifts. Often the most difficult seasons of our lives come with the greatest gifts and lessons. We have to have the right attitude and focus to see the gifts showered all over us every day. Wake up each morning with a positive attitude. All day long, look for the gifts and blessings bestowed upon you. At the end of the day, when your head hits the pillow, review all of the blessings you received that day. This gratitude habit takes literally seconds but has a huge impact on the quality of your life.

Your Life Is Your Work of Art

Do you remember when you were a little kid and you would have a big piece of white construction paper in front of you? You could create anything you wanted. But if you were anything like me, you drew the same picture over and over because you knew how to draw mountains, birds, trees, and flowers. The life you are living right now is your unique creation. Are you inspired and lit up by your life? Or are you choosing the path of least resistance? Are you daring to dream, or are you comfortable drawing the same M-shaped birds?

Get out a big white piece of paper and write at the top,

"In my dream world …." Write whatever comes to you. Don't sensor, just write.

Maybe you see yourself climbing Mount Everest or building wells for children in Africa.

Maybe you see yourself fit, lean, and full of energy and vitality.

Maybe you see yourself wise and confident, knowing exactly what to say in each situation.

Maybe you see yourself running a marathon or writing a New York Times bestseller.

Maybe you picture yourself living a life led by the Divine, where synchronicity and serendipity are your constant companions.

Maybe you visualize a home that is warm, cozy, and inspiring.

Maybe you dream of a close, tight, fun, good-to-each other family.

Maybe you picture money coming to you easily and often.

Maybe you want to be a person that is easy about things, with a sense that everything is always working out for you.

Maybe you dream of travelling the world.

Maybe you dream of being comfortable in your own skin.

Maybe you dream of making an impact for good in this world.

Whatever your dream is, write it down. Flesh it out. Give it color and texture. Smell it. Taste it. See it clearly. The life you create is your gift to yourself, the world, and God. When we go back to Heaven and stand before God, we want to know we went big here on Earth. We went for it. Create the best life you possibly can in each moment.

Stop Pulling on the Leash

W hen I come home, our dog Bella is so excited she pulls on her leash frantically such that it makes it difficult to unleash her. I always tell her, "Just relax and I can get you off faster." This funny, daily ritual always reminds me of my own impatience. I'm sure God and my angels have thought the exact same sentiment toward me many, many times. This past Mother's Day, my kids all went in on a pair of Lululemon pants for me. A few days before Mother's Day, I came downstairs wearing the exact pants. My daughter was so upset that I had purchased the pants. She wanted to give me a gift she knew I would love. I didn't wait for it. I was worried the pants would sell out. I had no idea my kids had already purchased the pants for me.

When we effort too hard, we are like my dog pulling on the leash or me jumping the gun on the yoga pants. Our Western mentality is very masculine: Get it done. Make it happen. The feminine mentality is more patient. It creates the fertile soil that allows things to happen. Like most opposing forces, a combination of the two is magical. Prepare the soil, and then act from this inspired place. When we are aligned with God and our inner spirit, we follow our intuition, our inner knowing. Synchronicities and miracles become part of our daily experience. The inspiration to take a particular path leads us to the perfect connection. We wake up from a much needed nap or meditation with a problem solved. Ideas come to us while walking our dogs, laughing at a sitcom, or washing our hair. Life becomes easier. We are guided by the Divine rather than our egos.

You can use a meat cleaver to cut a piece of cake, but it is so much more elegant and efficient to use a cake knife. When we force things to happen, the vibration being offered is control and scarcity. When we allow things to happen in perfect timing, the vibration being offered is trust and faith. The next time you catch yourself pulling hard on the leash, stop, relax, take a deep breath, and lift the situation to God. Changing this one habit will create a peace in your life like no other.

Nugget #17

A Legacy of Kindness

The legacy I want to leave on this Earth is very clear to me. I want people to remember the kindnesses I showed them. I want them to remember how they felt in my presence. I want people to remember feeling heard and understood, without a trace of judgment. The small acts of love we bestow on one another will be our greatest source of pride and satisfaction from this life. When I go to Heaven and watch the video of my life, I want to see hundreds and hundreds of big, but mostly small acts of love and kindness that came from me. I want to experience the feelings the receiver felt. This is why we come to Earth. To give and receive love. We get so distracted here, but it's really quite simple. No matter what kind of work you do for a living, find ways to spread love and kindness every day. Think about your last day on this planet and how you want people to describe you. Are you living each day right now in a way that will have those words spoken about you? Do you reach out and help whenever you can? Are you the first one to say, "Hello" or "I'm sorry?" Do you listen with your heart when someone is hurting? Do you give to people who you know can never repay you? Ask God first thing in the morning to show you where you can be a blessing to someone today. At the end of the day when you put your head on your pillow, review the moments you were able to be a blessing. I promise that God will show you where you were a blessing, and you will receive blessings in return. The two go together. You can't give without receiving. It's a law.

One Final Nugget

My final nugget is that our individual thoughts are the building blocks for our entire lives. The greatest skill we can ever learn is the ability to master our thoughts. Most people have a negative topic on which they ruminate. For some it's their body. For others it's their spouse or their bank account. Sometimes people focus on behavior they would like to change in another. Giving more airtime or attention to the unwanted does not bring the wanted into our lives. I have a list of "good feeling thoughts" I run through my mind as I walk my dog early in the morning. They are something like this:

I sure love this walk. I love the trees, the sound of the birds chirping, the green grass.

I love where I live.

I love that I have the ability to walk.

I love this little dog that gives so much joy and love to my family.

Think good feeling thoughts early in the day and then listen to any intuitive whispers you may receive. You may take a different route because of a divine whisper and run into an old friend that says the exact thing you need to hear. It all begins with a single thought. Focusing on positive, good feeling thoughts is a skill that takes time. But as you progress, you will be able to hold yourself in a good feeling place for longer and longer. This is when true miracles will start to happen in your life. So begin today. Right now in this moment.

June 7, 2009 was a death and a birth. As my dad took his final breath in my home, he breathed life into this book, a story he wanted me to share. I pray the words written here will bless you in positive and profound ways.

*I would like to thank Richard Kaufman for donating his professional editing services for this book.